Late Words
Poems — 1976

Compliments of:
Estate of Janet Piper
P.O. Box 474
Huntsville, TX 77342-0474

Late Words
Poems — 1976
by
Janet Piper

Acknowledgement is due the Houghton-Mifflin Company for permission to quote several lines and phrases from "Voyage To The Moon"; "Long Hot Summer"; "A Good Man In A Bad Time"; "Night Watch In The City of Boston"; and "Definitions Of Old Age" by Archibald MacLeish (New and Collected Poems, 1976); also for four lines from "Nocturne"; the eight opening lines of "The Hamlet of A. MacLeish"; and for several lines from "Reasons For Music" (Collected Poems, Sentry Edition 30, 1962); as well as for several lines from the prose play, Scratch (1971), and for the epigraph to the present volume, from A Continuing Journey (1968).

Acknowledgement is made of a quotation of five sentences from The Americans vol. II, page 362, by Daniel Boorstin, Vintage Books (v-358).

Thanks are also due for a quotation of four lines from "Blight On Elm" by Daryl Hines (The New Yorker, September 13, 1976).

First Printing, 2004

Estate of Janet Piper
P.O. Box 474
Huntsville, TX 77342-0474

Introduction

In the years immediately following her retirement from teaching (1972), Janet Pressley Piper took up again the pleasure and joy of writing poetry. She re-discovered what had been her earliest literary impulse, and, at long last, she had the time and leisure to indulge her fondest passion. And, most importantly, as she carefully reviewed poems written in her youth, she became convinced that she possessed a considerable poetic gift which had too long lain dormant because of personal tragedies and professional responsibilities.

It is not too much to say that this realization of literary ability and worth became the animating force of the twenty five years of her life following retirement. With a vigor beyond her years, she entered a new creative period, one which lasted almost literally to her death. True, her physical health declined over the last two decades of her life, but her mental acuteness never failed. She possessed something approaching total recall, and, as the confines of her physical world grew smaller, her mental world expanded and extended itself to embrace literature, philosophy, art, history, science, and politics.

Significantly, it was the relationships between literature and politics that most clearly dominated her thinking and her poetry in the mid-1970's, the time of the writing and collecting of *Late Words*.

Central to her entire artistic vision and her assessment of political developments during her long lifetime was the belief that far too often American literary figures of the early to mid-twentieth century had supported authoritarian regimes designed to stifle human freedom and keep most people in a semi-medieval relationship with church and state. Eliot, Pound, and others were to her reprehensible individuals whose disdain for the common man and trust in fascist leaders made them abhorrent rather than admirable. She had herself attempted to expose this "Modernist Conspiracy" in 1949 by writing a book with the initial encouragement of W. H. Auden. However, Auden withdrew his support when he discovered that her "thesis" rebuked modern writers rather than affirmed them. Auden's "betrayal" caused untold personal pain for Piper, but it strengthened her determination to reveal the truth about artistic modernism.

Many of the poems in this volume should be read in the light of her "thesis," and others, including the short play, reflect Piper's grief over the (to put it in the best light) ambivalent attitude of Archibald MacLeish toward America and the future of a democratic society.

MacLeish, whose privileged background and native genius gave him all that was necessary to become a great American scholar who supported the people, spent, from Piper's point of view, a depressingly large amount of his career praising the likes of Eliot, Yeats, Pound, and other anti-democratic writers. She believed that he, as well as they, would have been more pleased with an Axis victory in World War II than an Allied one, since they all had the misguided notion that only an authoritarian state, unified and stratified, could produce great art. They believed authority in church and state would "save civilization," by which they meant the dominance of art and theology. Piper, in exasperation, would exclaim, "They did it for what they believed was a good cause!" That was for her the cruelest irony of the Modernist agenda.

Late Words is perhaps best seen as a collection of literary works calling on America's hubristic literary elite to abandon its endorsement of totalitarian politics, to absolve itself of the guilt of its too generous praise of fascistic literary and political ideas, and to return American literature to the appropriate celebration of democratic vistas.

Dr. David S. Gallant
May, 2004

Seven years are now elaps'd dear rambling volume
Since to all knavish wights, a foe,
sent you forth to vex and gall 'em,
Or drive them to the shades below!

This I can say, you've spread your wings afar,
Hostile to garter, ribbon, crown, and star;
Still on the people's, still on Freedom's side,
With full determin'd aim, to baffle every claim
Of well-born wights, that aim mount and ride.

Philip Freneau
(from To My Book — 1795 Edition)

An American. . .cannot permit himself to
believe that it takes courage to tell the
truth in this republic. To believe that would be
to believe that the enemies of American freedom
have already destroyed it and that the herd now
rules.

Archibald MacLeish
(from A Continuing Journey)

Table of Contents

Exorcism

Put off
The worldly mask!
Be deaf
To worldly chatter --
The world's clatter.

Remove
The perilous stuff
Of brain,
Of bosom!
What will remain

Of the organism,
The mechanism?
Consciousness?
Yes --
Dig deeper!

Lift
The last layer --
What is left?
Sentience?
Yes --

More aware,
More acute, more alive
Than before --
More swift
Than ever!

To put off love
And worldly wish
Is not enough:
Of these bereft,
What is left?

What is still
To discover,
Decipher,
Uncover?
Life.

Exorcism

OLD PEOPLE

I

The old ladies choose
Last illusions
To live with and die by.

They chatter and nod
As their bubble visions fly by --
Of themselves -- of the world -- of God.

They don't see or hear very well,
So they really can't tell
They share no agreement at all.

Illusion is all they have
To call their own --
Leave them alone!

So also old men.

II

"Only the old know Time --
      They feel it flow
Like water through the fingers.
      When the light
Ebbs from the pasture,
      They wade
In night, and are afraid."

Afraid?
      Afraid of what?
Of a past
      That never was?
Of a present that is not?
      No, but that secret of the dark --
The heart knows.

TWELVE QUATRAINS

I

Life is an endurance test
    For most men and women:
Some fall behind or pass the rest;
    None win.

II

Misery is a human sea --
    If you can't swim and have no boat,
Learn to tread water, or wade it:
    You can't evade it.,

III

The human lot -- at life's end -- face it:
    The sum of faith and belief
Is grief, grief, grief...
    To accept is not to embrace it.

IV

Patience -- courage -- fortitude --
     Are words ill understood:
Until made good
     In fact and deed -- mere platitude.

V

I wear my heart upon my sleeve
     Quite naked and bare -- look it over!
Would yours look cleaner, better, braver,
     Worn like this -- without cover?

VI

About the heart and the way you wear it:
     If exposed, immunization,
Cauterization, sterilization
     Will fit you to bear it.

VII

No one thinks my "work" important --
     Not even I!
If it is not, whose is? Name names, show me faces --
     Explain to me why.

VIII

Think as you please, say what you will!
　　When this book is read
I may well be dead
　　Or, if not that, then senile.

IX

Some people are mean, because they were hurt,
　　Some are mean, because they were not:
One tends to be defensive
　　Lest these prove offensive.

X

"Initiates" think they are clever and virtuous,
　　The "happy few" who are "human" and "care" --
Questioned, "Why be obnoxious? Why hurt you us?"
　　They merely stare.

XI

Neither optimist nor pessimist --
    Cautious, rather, and wary,
Secretive in her happiness:
    "Sad is the mask of merry".

XII

"God intended the earth for praise --
    Why else its beauty?"
So the poet as official guide: but, in an aside
    "I am only doing my duty."

"MEANING" AND THE MOON

I

". . wanderer in her sky,
a wonder to us past the reach of wonder,
a light beyond our lights, our lives, the rising earth,
    a meaning to us,
                0, a meaning!"
        -- A. MacLeish "Voyage To The Moon"

Well, it could "mean"
That the old planet shrank
Until we outgrew her --
Or, perhaps, that we found
A place to escape to,
In the event that we blew her.

Perhaps a "meaning" is
That poets should, belatedly, defer
To science, technology, and the computer --
Speak less of the "diminishment" of man,
Bear more in mind The "giant leap of humankind".

The scientists' gain is not
The poets' loss,
Though it may seem so;
We may be forgiven If we indulge in a
Little nostalgia
On the poets' behalf and our own!

            ...

    "Full moon, moon-rise,-the old pain
    Of brightness in dilated eyes -- "

"Why do we stand
To watch so long the fall of moonlight on
the sand?"

"What is it we cannot recall?"
...

From these night fields and waters do men raise
Sailors from ship, sleepers from their bed,
Born mortal men and haunted with brief days,
Their eyes to that vast silence overhead.
They see the moon walk slowly in her ways
And the grave stars and all the dark outspread:
They raise their mortal eyelids from the ground,
Question it...
            What art thou? ...
                  And no sound.

II

(In 1969 after the flight of Apollo Eight, the poet wrote these
lines one is happy to paraphrase.)

To see the rising earth, small,
            Oval, beautiful,
Balancing its blue shell --
            One in a galaxy of motes

In that eternal sea
            Of silence where it floats
Riders, Brothers -- what are we
            Adrift in that infinity?

THE MEANING OF EVOLUTION
(After hearing Prince Philip on the Galapagos Archipelago)

The followers of Charles Darwin
Confirm his answers to the "How", the "When";
But ah! to that hardest word, the "Why?",
Even the marine iguana
Has no reply.

ODD ANTIPHONY

Unlike the mountain
And the squirrel,
Emerson and Emily
Had no quarrel.

She might concede, if queried,
That she fitted into place
Notes
That other poets dropped,

But not
That she picked up,
And buried,
Fallen nuts.

Still, in her poems,
One may sometimes hear
An overtone
Of Emerson.

THE OLD LOCALS

Were the old New England poets stupid --
Emerson, Dickinson, Whitman, Thoreau?
Was there something they knew that the "in" poets do not,
Or something crucial they did not know?

Emerson, who prayed and left the church,
When Ellen Tucker's inheritance
Made it feasible to practice, as to preach,
Independence and self-reliance.

Thoreau, who, "famous with his God",
Sought no worldly fame abroad;
Who strong in faith, upright and moral,
Disdained to barter for the laurel.

Whitman, whose tenderness to young
Dead soldiers, suggests necrophilia,
Not to be stressed
In poetic memorabilia.

Emily, who conferred upon herself the degree,
Empress of Calvary,
Feared of robin, daffodil, and bee
Lèse majesty.

The deep woods poems
Are among Frost's best,
As we all know,
But where is Frost now?

The thrush calls still
From the pillared dark --
Pure song -- indifferent.
Frost has gone where the music went.

VERBAL BEHAVIOUR

I

Behind the eyes,
Not quite
Awake,
Colors, images,
Shifting shapes
Take
Form,
And patterns
Make.

The bright
Words,
Like birds
In flight,
Dart, alight,
Uprise,
Illuminate
The night.
O, lovely light!

II
The butterfly and bee
Extract
Their substance
From the flower;
The honey
On the poet's tongue
Is borrowed
From another's song.

To make
Meaning of music,
Music
Of meaning,
Is the poet's dower:
And all the power
Of the poetic
Act.

III
Aiken, Yeats,
MacLeish,
Eliot --
Global, cosmopolitan,
Polyglot:
They are not good,
They are not great.
They invite
One's hate;
And yet,

One owes them
A debt:
In Auden's words,
Time "worships
Language,

And forgives
Every one
By whom it lives"...
Pardons all
For writing well.

IV

Does the mind roused from "fishing in some weedy deep",
    Remember the bird, the reef, the sea-beat?

Or, sometimes, lapsing into sleep
    Where drowned dreams meet,

Hearing the night sound of the words for "always",
    "Ever", "forever" -- recall

That saddest of all words -- that sea-swung-knell,
    "Farewell...farewell"?

V

The grub, tight-wound,
In darkness bound,
Emerged and found
Radiant wings with which to fly --
    With which to fly!

Fragile, ephemeral,
Casual miracle,
It does not rise high;
It will fall to the ground;
    Soon it will die

Even as I -- even as I!

"BEYOND FREEDOM AND DIGNITY"

I

The rewards "sought him",
  As Skinner said they did,
(And Emerson affirmed that they would.)
  Lawyer, "statesman," administrator,
Honors were laid at his feet --
  And the world pronounced them meet.

The poet's reward is fame,
  And, in abundance, it came,
But of his poetic progeny,
  Though sound in wind and limb,
Few satisfied him:
  Where place the blame?

As between "genetic endowment"
  And "pressures of environment";
That is, "Fortune's arrows and slings",
  Environment wins hand over fist.
Let Skinner pursue his experiment
  And "humanists" cease to resist.

Judging from personal experience,
  And what one has observed:
Few receive the rewards they've deserved;
  Fortune may "favor the brave",
But "more" still comes to those who have --
  Let poetry yield now to science.

II

I have just "had"
A book of poems
And I feel "good",
As even Mr. Skinner
Agrees that I should.

I provided a <u>locus</u>
Where they could grow;
Did an apple tree father them
That I might gather them?
It would really seem so.

Like the hen which has just
Laid an egg,
I am allowed to cluck
At my good luck,
As Butler said, a proper hen must.

III

Yet Hopkins has well stated
The case for an opposing view:
The "mind"; he says, is "mother of immortal song".
Nine months -- nine years-- he waited
While his songs gestated.

Many, no doubt, were never created,
Lacking that "sweet fire", the "muse's sire,"
"The strong spur" like "blow-pipe flame";
Lacking that "fine delight
That fathers thought" — the fleeting insight.

Hopkins' mind "had mountains" yet provided a locus
Where Shelley and Scotus
Could merge;
"Love from its awful throne of patient power
In the wise heart, from the narrow verge

"Of crag-like agony, springs
And folds over the world
Its healing wings."
Hear Hopkins: "And though the last lights
Off the black West went,

Oh, morning at the brown brink
Eastward, springs —
Because the Holy Ghost over the bent
World broods with warm breast
And with ah! bright wings."

IV

As to whether
It is the itch
Of our grandfather
We scratch
Or our own;

Or whether or not
It is our lot
To play "sweating Sisyphus",
Perpetually
Rolling the stone,

We might again
Cite Emerson,
Who never heard of genes
But took to task
His "spendthrift sires."

"Bad husbands of their fires",
Who failed to provide
The sinews and thews,
The physical means,
To bring to fruition their seed.

V

We may well agree
That we are not free,
Lack dignity,
Yet still protest
(With Henry Beston)
We are neither sheep nor rats.

Animals
Are not metaphors
For man's
Degradation,
Subject to his patronization:
They are not ours.

"They are their own nations --
Prisoners caught
Like ourselves, in the net
Of time and birth,
Of life on earth":
Not to be "measured" by man!

VI

Peter Shaw has written a book on John Adams' character
(Which I do not intend to read),
But I have seen several reviews
Which, although they are not new
Summarize interesting views.

Adams himself said that a desire
For the attention and congratulation
Of one's fellowmen is the "great spring
Of social action". It is ambition
Draws men -- that and a longing for fame.

Adams waged a continuing battle to translate
These flaws of character into drives
He could acknowledge and accept
In himself without shame --
A passion for achievement and distinction.

This struggle to make virtue of vices
Is what gives Adams' personality
Its particular intensity,
According to Shaw, holding in check a
Thirst for revenge and a tendency to vanity.

John Adams, it seems, had the luck
To be "in the right place at the right time".
His "precarious personal equilibrium"
Did not forestall his success
As it might, otherwise, have done.

In a recent election, an unknown John Adams
Won handily on the strength of the name --
The same which defeated John Adams' descendants,
The embittered Brooks and Henry, who, repudiated
By "the people", repudiated them,

And so provided a precedent
For our century's fascist sympathizers, ex-patriates,
With equally famous names;
As also for such a notorious press-agent
As Pound who equates

The Adams' views
With his own,
And those
Of his hero,
Il Duce.

VII

B.F. Skinner in <u>Particulars of My Life</u>, explaining the
    attraction
Of an authorial career and its renunciation,
Analyzes what he considers its motivation:
He is convinced that the "desire to write"
Resolves itself into an "instinct" essentially "mean".

Whether it be lust of money or flesh,
The urge to be known as a genius, the wish,
"To see one's name in the paper",
Or some mystical desire to "express oneself",
The "artist" has much in common with the liar.

Skinner doesn't "exactly condemn the desire",
But he would have it made clear;
Strip it of spurious glamor,
Illusionary grandeur, discounting
The "artist's" extravagant claims,

And fine-sounding metaphorical names:
"Saviours" and "seers";
"Soothsayers" --
"Unacknowledged legislators";
"Antennae of the race".

Perhaps, when young, one was carried away
By this view and inclined to share it,
But sobered by life at seventy-five
One concedes to Skinner's argument
Some merit.

The athlete increases his skills,
The racer of motors his speed;
The avid business man,
The keen politician,
Their power over money and men.

So the poet enhances
His gift for words,
If fate or fortune affords
The requisite chances
For cultivation, practice, rewards.

VIII

"Not all lovers of music
        Want to write music,
Not all lovers of poetry
        Want to write poetry",
The poet has said in prose.

"But, for some, the love is such
        That the only satisfaction in life
Is to pursue it, and though
        I don't understand it,
I am one of those."

No one need question
        The strength or depth
Of his devotion:
        Many volumes attest
The long pursuit and the quest.

We have the poet's sanction for disavowing
        Violent polemic and strenuous rhetoric
Of earlier days,
        As in the "middle period"
Poems and plays.

As, also, perhaps, for disallowing
        The extravagant praise
Of "Poetry Power" in "In Challenge
        Not Defense",
And other such essays.

In later "wrestlings with the angel"
        "The Infinite Reason" or "Reasons
For Music", one listens --
        At some distance --
With sympathy, awe, respect.

But in such spontaneous flight
        As "They Come No More
Those Birds,
        Those Finches",
One shares the delight.

He speaks of "the labor of order"
    And its purpose: "To impose
On the confused, fortuitous
    Flowing away of the world,
Form" -- structure, repose.

Or, more magniloquently:
    "To build the Acropolis of Eternity
That crumbles again and again is my task.
    The heart's necessity compels me:
Marx I am: poet must be."

And me? Am I a poet? I am not compelled
    To build or rebuild Acropolis --
Whether in time or eternity,
    However often they crumble.
I am a woman; is my task, then, more humble?

IX

No one knows
Why the wind blows
Or what moves
The waves
Of the sea --
Least of all, me --
Who have just "had"
This poetry.

May not I,
In my ignorance,
Like Emerson, suppose
The self-same power

Which brought together
Poet and flower,
That "rival of the rose"
Brings me?

Or that the "love
Which moves the sun
And other stars",
Moved Dante once,
And Emerson--
And now, Skinner, MacLeish,
And me?

THE MOUNTAINS OVER PERSIA

I

To reanimate the dead
To perform "neurodramas", recite
Chilling, ambiguous poems
In a stone amphitheater,
Reminiscent of the Greek
For a captive audience;
Conditioned creatures, masked,
Deprived of sentience.

    Why?

In the science fiction thriller,
The old mage, when asked,
Solemnly asserts:
"The snake-like coldness of men's hearts,
In past or future time,
Is the ultimate crime...
I would make them weep --
I will one day."

Why?

II

Those who recall
        Robert Graves' poem, "The Laureate",
A tribute to the integrity
        Of Robert Bridges,
Will remember the image
        Of the old poet, staring straight
Into the sun, speaking his "old-fashioned" mind,
        In The Testament of Beauty.

In "The Old Man and The Lizard", a later poet,
        Translating and transposing the metaphor,
Questions the lizard, lover of light and heat,
        As to its secret:
Is it for love of the glory of sun and its gold
        That he stares with impunity
At that flame, annihilating and blinding,
        Or because his heart -- like his blood -- is cold?

MARK VAN DOREN AND THE DIALOGUES

Questioned <u>re</u> "Invitation To Learning" in 1942,
As to whether he was neo-Thomist or not,
Van Doren's answer was flat:
"I am no more one of those things
Than I am a tom-cat",
Which, for the time being, had to be that.

In 1949, in the "summer of fear",
When off to the north, "the woods were on fire",
What would he have said of cats and trees?
In the mini-candor of the <u>Dialogues</u>,
(Recorded and televised in 1968),
He discourses at length on the second of these.

I remember a poem of yours
Which talks about the differences
Between the maple and the elm -- my favorite trees,
By the way, as you know --
The maple holding itself against the wind,
The elm tree letting go.

"All my experience concentrated in that drop
Of statement -- perhaps fifty words in the poem as a whole --
The breath-taking brevity of your lines!"
The poet only says, savoring the praise,
"Breath-taking brevity
Is a wonderful phrase."

"There are those who might say that this
Is an inconsequential subject; I don't think so.
Trees are a subject as much as a proposition is,
And that, too, is all right in poetry.
You can write a poem to say a given thing --
Something you think the public ought to want to know".

(Ah, that question of the poet and the public --
What is the poet's duty? The public's due?
Or that of the players in the prize games on television?
How measure the relative guilt of poet-father and player-son?
The beech "oaring upstream" -- the elm "all Ophelia in the
           moat of air"...
Would he have the public believe these are "merely trees"?)

"I was reading you last night,
And, frankly, I have been for days --
That line at the end of a poem in <u>Actfive</u>,
'If autumn ended and the cold light came',
The whole thing is wonderful but suddenly that last line --
It's like a signing off in music, a closing chord.

"Who wrote that poem? What is it called?"
"Well", the author said, "Winter is Another Season", and smiled.
"Or rather, 'Winter is Another Country'.
That shows What a good memory I have". (If they pretend
The poem concerns only the end of a season,
Not of an illicit love, they have, of course, their reason.)

Van Doren speaks of the supreme delight
Of having written a line one loves to recite.
"Oh, the greatest delight in the world", his friend agrees.
"To have written a line or lines
The world will not willingly forget, defines,
Might not one say, the true poet?"

"The greatest poets have been wise
In the sense that most men are not.
Shakespeare knew things no one else knew
Or knew only in a different way."
Van Doren reminds the poet of the "summer of fear",
Recalls the "sad smell of smoke in the air".

"The smell of burning leaves relates to the general experience:
The poem should be read in a psychological -- not a
metaphorical -- sense."
Leaving this vein, Van Doren says, "There's a strong fragrance
Of skunk lying here. Do you find it attractive?
What does it do to you? I rather like it."
To which the poet replies, "So do I. I like strong smells."

"THEY ALSO SERVE"

His state is kingly.
"Be", says he,
"A man -- like me --
American and free!"
He would rule by fiat.

Words do what he wills.
He excels In all skills,
In games and exercise;
He passes for wise.

Lesser mortals come and go
At his desire;
Obey, bow low,
Move backward in awe;
Shamed, withdraw;

Keep quiet.
Few venture a challenge
Or risk his sneer
At cowards who don't dare
Speak out, seek "revenge"!

"Like fools
You forgather. You follow each other
Like bleating sheep! Rats in vats!",
He orates, maligning the animals
To denigrate men.

He cites Holmes, a "great man"
Who "taught the human herd
How liberty is won
By man alone --
Minority of one."

He foresees the wreath
To be placed
On his bust
At his death --
Unofficial laureate.

They also serve. They wait.

"HEROES AND HERO-WORSHIP"

I

The President's wife
    Invited me to tea
To discuss, as she said,
    My philosophy.

"The Young need heroes!
    Let us have no debunking chatter;
Of Wordsworth's natural daughter --
    Or other such matter."
           . . .

Forty years later I read
    A summation, by the praiser of Pound,
In praise of another "good" man whom he "loves",
    Of what the Young need:

"Competent friends", bold men
    Who won't "run out", "quit the venture",
"Sell up the country", rob it blind --
    "Write off mankind."

Discreetly, he doesn't mention
    <u>Der führer</u>, <u>il duce</u>, or Lenin,
Nor precisely express his intention;
    What does he really "mean"?

"The American journey", he says, "has not ended,"
    "America is never accomplished, always growing.
"The West is a country of the mind, and so eternal"...
    "America is West and the wind blowing".

II

Good and evil are four-letter words,
        (As, likewise, love and hate), engines of action:
Young poets, good or bad, poor or rich,
        "Feel" that they know
Which is which,
        And choose their faction.

Young artists grow bolder,
        Acquire reputation,
Identify with their views:
        Too soon they are older
And, through habit or pride, refuse
        Retraction.

Picasso, Stravinsky,
        Nietzchean progeny,
Affronted public ear and eye:
        Mistaking persistence
For courage,
        Prolonged the outrage.

III

"The expression 'my country' in America had meant my
colony or my state long before it meant anything else. Even in
the early 19th century, to John Adams it still meant
Massachusetts and to Jefferson it meant Virginia. These local
loyalties -- and local prejudices -- were the first raw material
not only of an American patriotism, but of an American
history."
                                        ...

"The Adams-Tudor version of Otis and of the origins of the Revolution was perpetuated in Boston's Fourth of July Orations, which were made into a book and given by a patriotic Bostonian to every school in the city, every academy in the state, and every college in the United States."
-- Daniel Boorstin

"The poets write the histories,
        Create the heroes"; the poet said,
"Turn history back into myth;
        Reanimate the dead"

If Virginia could deify Washington,
        Patrick Henry, Richard Henry Lee,
In 'plaster of Paris' and prose,
        "There are those

In New England", said John Adams,
        "Who can also use
'Panegyric and hyperbole',
        Purple embroidery

To aggrandize and celebrate
        James Otis and other such heroes
Through textbook and oration,
        They exaggerate and perpetuate

Their own version
        Of the American Revolution!
"Mother of the great Republic!"
        "Mother town!" "City of Man!"

In Massachusetts,
       Let them have their say,
But repeat it not
       In Virginia!

IV

Let this "faceless public"
       Which you accuse,
For once, make response
       To this abuse.

"This is John Adams'
       Holy Land."
"Whose land?"
       "He would see you damn'd."

"You would make me hate
       This ghost from the past, an enemy,
Stuffed down my throat
       By the media and Mellon money".

"City of the famous dead
       Where Otis spoke
And Adams' heart was bred. .
       "City of Man!" "City of Greed!"

"Mother of the Great Republic,
       Mother town -- !"
Oh, come on!
       Come off it! Come down!

BICENTENNIAL

I

What could one expect
        Of such a project,
Funded by Mellon money,
        But tongue-in-cheek
Speech -- shallow, hollow,
        And suspect?

What would one wish
        Of the poet, MacLeish?
Not merely rhetoric,
        However lyric,
Learned, didactic --
        Not pretentious pastiche!

II

An old woman's voice
        From out the crowd
Now sounds aloud:
I have learned as I lived --
        Best like lemmings
        Rejoin the sea!
You have only one freedom

Only one choice --
    You are free not to be!

Leave to the leaders
    Their oratory,
Minatory, hortatory,
Ultimately nugatory.
    With none to listen,
    None to address --
None to follow, none to oppress,
Let the noble leaders create
    Their perfect State!

III

BILL MOYERS' JOURNAL
(Sunday, March 7, 1976)

BILL MOYERS' JOURNAL
Americans should celebrate the Bicentennial with a "humble sense of gratitude to whoever God is and wherever He is for the opportunity of self-government," says Pulitzer Prize winner Archibald MacLeish. Interviewed at his Connecticut home, the poet discusses his life and career. Included are MacLeish's recollections of his years in Paris with Hemingway, Picasso and other artists. (60 mm.)

(The Adams Living Room --
Jolly Adams and her brother,
Mrs. Murphy and her mother
Sit before the T.V. screen.)

Jolly: He's a poet -- we studied him at school.
He said, "A poem should not mean but be."
Our teacher said we had to listen!
Johnny has to listen, too.
It's an assignment!

Mrs. Adams: Well, I don't know...
Mrs. Murphy came over to watch "Return to
Peyton Place";
I wish we had two sets.
I don't know. .

Johny: Some assignment!
That guy she read from -- Professor Smith-- said,
"MacLeish is classical and aristocratic."
I thought Bill Moyers was democratic --
Why should he have him on?
Anyhow, I want to see the N.B.A. game on C.B.S.

Jolly: If you want a chance at a Basketball scholarship,
You better pass English! You listen!
Anyway, he knew Hemingway!
He lived in Paris. He had a yacht.
He had a weak knee -- I think he got it from football.
He knew a lot of sirens, too!

Mrs. Murphy: Well, he sounds kind of interesting.
          You all go ahead and listen --
          I don't mind.

Mrs. Adams: That's right nice of you, Mrs. Murphy --
          It's only an hour.
                    . . .
But here is Bill Moyers --
And with him, the poet,
Hardy, elegant, handsome,
(Slightly shrunken, somewhat lighter, Fighting a little shortness
of breath)
To do the honors of his country estate.
Not the squire in British fashion,
Nor, to be sure, <u>en grand seigneur</u>;
A Scottish laird? Not <u>quite</u> American --
(Oh, not an expatriate -- certified patriotic!)
Still, a trifle exotic,
In his skull-warming, jaunty berét.

Comfortably settled near one of the ponds,
Moyers questions the poet: What would he say
Of America's health at her bicentennial?

(Justifiably complacent, somewhat vain
Of his personal state of self-preservation))
Gracious, deprecatory, deferential,
Mr. MacLeish responds:
"Americans should thank God -- whoever or wherever
          He is --
For the opportunity to govern themselves" -- if they
          can, that is --

("The rights belong", he has said, in 'America Was
    Promises'
"To those who will take them".)
Does he still believe this?

Moyers doesn't ask -- but suggests, instead,
That he read from his newest radio play,
The Great American Fourth of July Parade
(Selected by International Poetry Forum, funded by the
    Mellon Foundation),
In which Adams and Jefferson review from their graves
Their hopes and fears for the new-born nation,
And express their reaction to present-day leaders and
    masses.
(This, the poet agreeably does -- and miraculously --
    without glasses.)
"They were not born", Jefferson said, "with saddles
    on their backs
For a favored few, booted and spurred, ready to ride" --
(Those riders that Yeats and his confréres
Would settle firm in their saddles again!)

"Yeats is the greatest poet since Keats",
Says MacLeish, "and his poem, 'The Second Coming'
Is the truest characterization of our time".
He permits two girls from "Parade" to hope
For "a different kind of revolution" (the Right kind?
    Yeats's kind?)
"Made by men -- for men -- with men to do the ruling after-
    ward" --
"Free men, proud and gentle in their freedom".
A black girl is allowed to say:

"Maybe Jefferson meant that liberty is still to win --
Is always still to win -- is always liberty -- "
(But the poet is not a naive girl! Did he speak
With his tongue in his cheek?)

For the rest, he has had, he says, a productive summer;
He will have a new book out next year.
He reads a poem from a group called "Family Album",
'The Grey Couple', a Joan and Darby pair,
And shows some family photographs --
Several of his wife and the well-known hero-brother,
Tragically killed in the First World War.
Yes, he has had his sorrow-- lost, besides, a son.
Still, he has been, he supposes, a fortunate man:
His wonderful marriage, his fame, the honors won!

...

A charming interview, in a charming setting,
With a charming eighty-three year old "smiling public man".
But when, at the last
He turns toward the vast
Invisible host,
His agonized stare,
The cavernous sockets betray
A mummied ghost,
Dessicated, lost --
The Huntsman, haunted, at bay.

Returned to his chair,
Waves of horror,
As spasms seize the lower jaw --

Cut! They are off the air!
But one saw --

(Lacrimae, lacrimae, lacrimae rerum!)

        (The Adams living room as before)

Jolly: Teacher said that the poet Yeats,
                Was called "King of the Cats",
                Like in the story by Stephen Benet.
                She read us a poem by MacLeish one day,
                About a cat in a wood that cried, "Farewell!"
                I guess it was under a spell.

Mrs. Adams: Well, Mrs. M.
                Our movie is still on --
                We can catch the last hour.

Johnny: What about me?
                I've missed my game --
                And all for nothing!
                I'm leaving.

Mrs. Murphy: His wife's right pretty --
                She looks nice, too.

Johnny: Like he says, he's been lucky --
                He's lived all over,
                And his wife left him free!
                How lucky can you be?

Jolly: It must have been hard
For her, sometimes, though --
Unless maybe she
Was glad to be free!
We don't know.
I wish I could be
Where he has been;
I wish I could see
What he has seen --
I'd remember it all!

Shall I turn on "Peyton Place"?
I'll watch, too.

In Philadelphia the other day, the distinguished Chief Justice of the United States of America --- speaking to new graduates of the University of Pennsylvania on the subject-of "What Do You Want from Your Century?" -- made a significant and complimentary reference to public television.

"Interviews," said Chief Justice Warren E. Burger; "such as that with Archibald MacLeish; the *Masterpiece Theatre; The Adams Chronicles*; the great operas, symphonies and ballets bring into every home treasures once reserved for the rich."

The End

IV

The age demanded and the age got
Its "prose cinema", its "mold in plaster",
Its prophet in cipher, its "modern master"
In the multi-masked expatriate,
The cosmic wonder, Eliot.

Lucky MacLeish, after near disaster,
Retrieves aplomb with a second shot,
Thanks to its sponsors and C.B.S. --
Introduced as "our unofficial laureate",
On Cronkite's "In Celebration of U.S."

Poised, cosmetically rejuvenated,
He gives us Adams and Jefferson recreated.
Spared the recurrence of spastic
Tremor, secure in his fame and glory at
Last, on film and tape at C.B.S -- a sculpture in plastic.

    (In "Parade," an old woman cries:
    "With private secrets and public lies!")

"A CITY ON A HILL"

> Virtue palters; Right is hence;
> Freedom praised, but hid:
> Funeral eloquence
> Rattles the coffin lid.
>   -- Ralph Waldo Emerson

Ronald Reagan, as reported in Newsweek,
    Driving between the blue Pacific
And the Santa Ynes mountains, remembering
    A time capsule in which his words
Would appear, was struck
    With an awful thought.

People, living when the capsule was read,
    Would know what the present generation
Had made of the nation:
    Would they still have our
Freedom? Would nuclear power
    Have destroyed half creation?

"The Republican platform displays our banner", he said,
    No bland pastel shades but bold
Unmistakable colors -- don't compromise!
    Don't get cynical --
Don't let your ideals grow cold!
    Don't let it down!

"There are millions and millions
    Of Americans out there
Who want to see
    A shining city on a hill --
Keep our party's feet to the fire,
    And, by heaven, they will."

KING FRAUD

"We may possibly survive
          Fraud in government,
But how could we live
          With fraud in art?
Fraud, in our time, is a form of government:"
          So far the poet in "The Venetian Grave",
And yet,
          One may inquire, "When was it not?"

But who is this Centennial Bell
          Which will not ring
And assures the people,
          "Fraud is King:"
Who is interlocutor?
          Who is auditor?
Who makes reply?
          Whose is the lie?

Who are "the people", treated like cattle,
          Seemingly born
To wear the rider's saddle,
          Bear his blows --
Who "deserve" what they get,
          And are always given
What they "deserve"
          By the master they serve?

And about the bell --
          Is it really a bell?
It may be a devil out of hell.
          There seems to be

A brimstone smell.
In <u>Scratch</u> we are given
A summary
Of his words and views.

"What is Liberty?
Some frontier idiot's
Foolish fantasy? -- "
With the wild geese for a paradigm;
They fly -- they fly
But which one knows why?
"Men are bullocks in a herd.
And Freedom? Freedom is a word."

"There is reality;
The other is dream;
Put them together
And you get what you have --
Your great Republic
Built on a rock,
Proof of belief,
Or monstrous fraud!"

But Lincoln was right;
They can fool some of the people
Some of the time, and some of them all the time,
But not all of them always.
A few know and knew --
Not all have disappeared,
And like Jefferson's word,
They <u>will</u> be heard!

POPULATION EXPLOSION

Let us have less talk
Of the fine
Georgian house and the vine --
More frank discussion
Of the real problem
And its possible solution,
By perfection of "the pill",
Vasectomy -- or abortion.

"Increase, multiply,
And replenish the earth"
May have served men well
On the bleak New England coast,
As in other times and places,
When none reckoned the cost
In expendable infants,
And a sex of inferior worth.

"The right to life of the unborn"
Makes a fine-sounding slogan
But life as a "right" is not qualified "good".
Until so assured and defined.
Let us have less pious agitation
By casuistical priests,
And sentimental
Or roboticized women.

FABLE OF THE CRITICS

I

The queer thing about it is
There wasn't <u>one</u> bird --
Or not <u>just</u> one bird --
There were, at least, two.

There was the pipit or warbler
Or plain citizen sparrow --
The finch or canary --
Any small passerine bird.

Then there was the death bird,
Vulture or seagull,
Eagle or cormorant,
Raven or crow.

Later came the shrike, the butcher bird,
An ominous third:
These combined to create
The great, great Dictator bird.

And the war was on!

II

For the veracious annals
Best consult other channels;
Hitchcock or some <u>echt</u> impresario.
But here, more or less,
Is the rude scenario:

There was this place
Called "Stupidity Street"
Where "singing birds sweet
Were sold in the shops
For the people to eat."

And who were these people?
Every one agreed
They were not very smart
(One poet addressed them <u>en masse</u>
As "Childheart".)

In time there would be
"The worm in the wheat,
And in the shops nothing
For people to eat --
Nothing for sale in Stupidity Street."

So the birds decided to organize
As the only possible solution.
They would wear a disguise
And not, advertise
An out-and-out revolution.

They didn't call it a strike
Or a let-down or sit-down,
Though it looked very like one:
They had a program and a manifesto
Which they announced with great zest:

In the "new" poetry
For the "people",
There would be
No melody.
(That was strictly for the birds!)

Poems might be palpable,
Possibly inaudible,
But always unintelligible,
Impenetrable,
Opaque.

Poetry must learn to be
Hideous and brutal,
Never beautiful,
"For", said Yeats,
"Beauty is difficult".

(But he very much approved
The esoteric and occult --
Or anything Chinese or, better, Japanese,
Or anything in Sanscrit or the Gaelic,
Or Byzantine Greek.)

Pound admired the Provencal,
Medieval Latin or burgeoning Romance.
(He wasn't understood at all,
For his Greek was Mycenean,
And his English pure Greek.)

Eliot's diction was impressive
But he made no sense when read.
He cited dark authorities
And stuffed the reader's head
"With ignorance not its own",

As Joel Barlow might have said.
But while we palavered,
The critics have fled;'
They weren't "real" critics, after all --
But only a part of the chorus led

By the great great Dictator bird.
Of whatever kind,
The birds are now flown --
But see the havoc they made!
Look at the lawn!

No wonder the guests
Couldn't agree
As to what they had heard
Or the kind of bird -
But the lines are redrawn.

And the war drags on...

THE ROCK, THE SEA, AND THE GULL

I

That boatload
Of bold adventurers
Sun-dazed, blood-crazed, blind --
Those latter-day Argonauts
Sailing upwind,
Seeking a sign,

Heard the shriek
From the bloody beak
Of the fabulous bird
On the topmost peak
Of the coral rock:
What did it mean?

Suffered the shock
Of the thundering wave
In the stone cave;
Beached the skiff;
Climbed the iron cliff,
Awed by the scene.

Were they betrayed
By something within,
(Dubbed by the bird Original Sin)?
Or gulled by a gull,
And the taste of daphne
In the brine?

1973

II

Praising the courage of Pablo Casals
    And of Beethoven,
The poet speaks of one's own.

I should like to pose him one question
    About the omission
From his latest collection

Of his poem, "The Rock In The Sea":
    Is it a too-transparent revelation
Of the "high Modernist" conspiracy?

As for my "reckless courage" and me,
    I include here my poem of '73,
"The Rock, the Gull, and the Sea".

These say less about gulls
Than about the conceit
Of our hubristic élite.

III

(<u>Apropos</u> "The Carrion Crow" --
on the suicide of
    F.O. Matthiessen)

There were martyrs in 1949
Of whom some lived.
I was one --
I survived:
Did you know?

We have also,
Our "American style"
Gulag Archipelago.
If you had known,
What would you have done?

Are you forgiven?
By me, certainly.
Christ is forgiveness
By definition.
Trouble not Heaven.

BALLAD

I

He sold his soul
For a prick of the thumb,
A place in the grove,
And a make-believe tomb;
A "bench-mark" above
The absolute sea.

Oh, is he a genius or isn't he?
Across the frontiers with the Supermen,
The Blood and the Brag would prove him so:
Having cast off pity, abolished remorse,
With Pound, Eliot, Yeats and Co.,
He still does not know.

<u>Oh, when will he know?</u>

II

Well, isn't he?
What is a genius anyway?
Consider the infant in his bed --
The talents and gifts which were shed

In profusion upon
His innocent head --
With what care he was nurtured
And educated!

Who could have guessed he would squander
His powers in too-generous praise
Of such poets as Baudelaire, Rilke, Perse, Pound, Eliot, Yeats,
To further a cause Half the world hates.
And many more would
If it were well understood.

Why? "God knows why!" We may ponder
With Megara, Herakles' reply:
"Would I have gone without the will
Of God to send me? Or his oracle?
I had his promise -- godhead -- the future --
All the future! Fame!"
That last infirmity -- risking reversal --
Fame! Fame! Infamy!

III

Let it be agreed --
The question of genius
May be conceded.
One needs only to reread,
As I did,
The earlier plays
To be struck
With the passionate power
In the occasional passage,
The moving rhythm,
The luminous phrase.

Dare I mention also
His comeliness,
In those days
When he served Luce and his "empire"?
There is a photograph,
In Swanberg's book
On that subject,
I had not seen before,
Which took
My breath,
With its beauty.

To be young, strong,
Greatly gifted,
And beautiful --
How could one's pride
Be satisfied

With trivial reward,
Not in accord
With the good
Already bestowed?
The best was deserved and desired:
Why not granted?

"Fame is no plant
That grows
On mortal soil,
Nor in the glistening foil
Set off to the world,
Nor in broad rumor lies
But lives and spreads aloft
By those pure eyes
And perfect witness
Of all-judging Jove" --
It was Fame he wanted.

"GOLDEN LADS AND GIRLS"

I

Golden lads and girls
Do not live
Happily ever after.

They forget
The laughter,
The ability, the sighing.

As in the emblem flower,
The gold turns grey,
The down blows away.

Growing old
Is a piecemeal leaving;
A letting-go:

The hands will not hold,
The limbs will not carry.
They scarcely know

When, in the grey evening,
They end their living,
Finish their dying.

II

Frost had boughten comfort
At his side
When he died.
To have a wifely nanny
Was the lucky lot
Of Britain's T.S. Eliot.

Luckier yet
The old poet --
Who ends his life,
Companioned by
The faithful wife
Who was his youthful bride.

REFLECTIONS ON IMMORTALITY

The old men raking the leaves in November,
Light as dead leaves, living only a little, remember
Their youth and their loves, the fame
Of the praisers of women, their despair
That the figures and faces were gone,
Though the words sounded.
They know now the dead die indeed; only the name,
Defenseless, inflated or wounded
By deceived or deceivers, lives on.

The words on the yellowing pages
Are soaked in the blood of strangers
Who gave the authors to drink,
Making them speak through the ages
Strange words in strange tongues,
Betraying their matter and meaning,
Pretending to say what they think:
Parasites or ghouls, still self-servers,
For money or fame, wasters of ink.

The dead live on, we are told, with the rest of us.
What do dead authors demand of the living?
What is the duty the living owe to the dead,
Failing which, they risk grave misfortune?

Thinking of their own deaths, the old men importune
The survivors -- lest the future be misled --
To judge them, as we all would be judged, by the best of us,
To weigh what they said, and were, and did, forgiving
The failures and faults, to praise the achieving.

The old men pronounce on gifted youth of earlier days;
Denounce Keats' own epitaph, proclaim him "misburied",
Misserved by "fatuous friends" -- for which, read Shelley,
That "honest maker", sublime elegist,
Whom the old men would have dismissed
As a "sniveling sentimentalist", his poetry
Aspersed as a "feeble self-pitying cry":
One need not malign Shelley, to give Keats praise,
The salvaged <u>cors cordium</u> traduced.

Emily Dickinson, too, deserves a better fate
Than to be made a cult object with which to beat
Talented women of our own day,
Elinor Wylie, Edna Millay,
With whom "male chauvinists" declined to compete,
But, willingly devious, combined to defeat.
Lay on Emily Dickinson's grave a wreath
For one who suffers a fame worse than death,
She who craved only, as final grace, the liberty to die.

Let Ezra Pound rest in his Venetian grave,
Until time, as it will, shall reveal
The truth that quibbles and quarrels conceal --
The kind and extent of the general treason
(For which Auden prayed Henry James' intercession),
In the intention and invention of "modernism",
And assess, in detail, the debt to Pound.
Time enough, then, to consider the mound
To be raised to his memory, by the gray sea in Italy.

1974

ULMUS AMERICANA

I

Time reports on the status of the battle:
The fungus borne by the black beetle,
Against the stately American elm.
Scientists have considered breeding
Armies of tiny parasitic wasps,
Coating the elms with beetle-attracting lure,
But Dupont has patented an insecticide --
A preventative -- though, alas! not a cure.

American poets have long celebrated the elm:
There is "The Dying Elm" by Philip Freneau
(Who had never heard of "Dutch elm blight",
Twentieth century "dirty tricks", Watergate, or Nixon):
"Lo! thy dejected branches die
Amidst the torrid air. Smit by the sun,
Thy withering leaves, that drooping hang,
Presage thine end approaching nigh."

"Man's the elm and Wealth the vine;
Stanch and strong the tendrils twine:
Though the frail ringlets thee deceive
None from its stock the vine can reave.
Fear not, then, thou child infirm

There is no god dares wrong a worm."
Thus Emerson -- whose logic escapes me,
Whether profound or naive.

In this week's <u>New Yorker</u>, Daryl Hines elegizes
"Our shady neighbors, familiars of the sun and rain,
Decimated by a radical disease",
And somewhat ingenuously, moralizes:
"This is how the suburbs lose their cool
By a coincidence never really strange,
The end in view is nearly natural,
The beautiful laid level with the plain".

II

Ah, but the lyrical
    Nostalgic, elegiacal,
Poet, life's end reverting
    To his true nature and ancestral --
Home, all-seeing, all-knowing
    Darkness of doom --

Who finds in the elm tree
    The obsessive symbol
Of all he had wished
    Might come to be --
No doubt had once been,
    Now lost irretrievably!

Lover of dark, seer in shadow,
    Never again will the sheltering elm
Offer him shade
    "Where the heart can see" --
Protect him at noon
    From the cruel sun.

The beetle of God is under the bark
And the age of the leafy tree is done:
the cities are dying one by one
of the heat and the hate and the naked sun.

Yet the will-to-believe
    May still deceive;
The Desperate grasp
    At the parasite wasp
And the black beetle lure;
    Or depend upon Dupont for cure.

"EARTH SONG"

I

Speaking for Earth, "Where are the old men?"
Asked Emerson,
"Haranguing the nation!
Born with a gift of words,
What should they do with it
But make an oration?
Had you lived longer
You would have heard
Them recite on television."

"Where are the heritors...
"Fled like the flood's foam...
 "The lawyers and the laws...
"Clean swept here from...
 "Everyone wanted to stay and is gone."
"Those who ruled,
Or aspired to,
Hold now no power --"
"But I do; I hold them."

II

It was dark in the room where he was made,
    The light bones knit together,
But he was lulled and unafraid:
    It was dark in the womb of his mother.

The flesh and the heart
    Decay, wash away, dissever;
The intricate bones fall apart:
    It is dark in the womb of that other.

III

In that dark of earth
As in dark before birth,
    He will lie alone.

He need not fear the rising sun,
The burning noon --
    He will not wake too soon.

"FEAR NO MORE THE HEAT OF THE SUN"

I

The worldly task is done;
Death's destiny unknown,
As also Life's wages.

Purge the pride
Of old despair,
Old pain,

Heal the hurt
That on the heart
So long has lain.

Before the ritual of dawn,
Before the dark
Is gone,

Prepare
The lidless eyes,
The deafened ear

To bear
The full diapason
Of the blazing sun.

Receive this prayer.

II

Not for "magic casements
　　Opening on the foam
Of perilous seas
　　In faery lands forlorn."

No! But for the transparent pane
　　Through which one sees
And the gift of sight:
　　One is grateful for these.

As for that bird
　　Which too early,
Too soon,
　　Caroled the dawn,

It is gone --
　　It has flown
Straight into the sun --
　　The burning day!

"Who are you and where are you going?"
"I am an old woman on the way to her dying."

"Old woman, old woman, why do you hurry?
Death comes soon enough. Such meeting

"Has never been merry --
Why hobble to greet him?"

"I would catch in a phrase
The red-bud's roseate haze,"

"The japonica's radiant blaze
Before the flowers' falling.

"The pink magnolia tree
I came abroad to see

"Is even now strowing
The ground with its rose-mauve snowing!

"The camellia's brief perfection
Urges me on --

"I hear the spring calling!"